TOXIC TRENDS

BY MADLYN HAMBLIN & CARI HAUS

Pacific Press Publishing Association
Boise, Idaho
Oshawa, Ontario, Canada

Edited by Jerry D. Thomas
Cover design by Michelle C. Petz
Alarm clock, DC, and television images © 1995
PhotoDisc, Inc.

The author assumes full responsibility for the accuracy of all facts and quotations cited in this book.

ISBN 0-8163-1336-9

96 97 98 99 00 · 5 4 3 2 1

TABLE OF CONTENTS

Foreword   5

Introduction   7

For the Reader   11

Chapter 1: **Tied to the Tube**   16

Chapter 2: **The Electronic Escape**   28

Chapter 3: **The Digital Decade**   41

Chapter 4: **You Are What You Read**   50

Chapter 5: **Life in the Twilight Zone**   59

Chapter 6: **The Pick-Me-Up That Always Lets You Down**   66

Chapter 7: **The Power to Change**   74

DEDICATION

For my children,
KRISTY AND MICHAEL,
who patiently listened in their growing-up years
to the principles stated in Philippians 4:8:
"Finally, brethren, whatsoever things are true,
whatsoever things are honest, whatsoever things
are just, whatsoever things are pure, whatsoever
things
are lovely, whatsoever things are of good report; if
there be any virtue, and if there be any praise, think
on these things."

Madlyn Hamblin

DEDICATION

For my children,
MICHAEL AND MATTHEW,
who are still very young,
for being so sweet, loving, and supportive.
May they learn the principles of Philippians 4:8.
And to my husband,
DAVID,
for being my best friend
(and watching the kids so I could write this book!).

Cari Haus

FOREWORD

The moral fabric of society is coming apart. Values once cherished are discarded like hand-me-downs from another generation. Moral standards have sunk to a new ebb. The new freedoms and permissiveness of our society have produced their harvest. Teenage suicide is at an all-time high. Marriages are falling apart. Antidepressants have become the drug of choice of the 1990s. Mass media with its illicit sex and rampant violence has crippled the minds of our generation. What can be done?

The book you hold in your hands not only analyzes the trends in our society but presents practical solutions. Madlyn Hamblin and Cari Haus have something to say, and they say it well. *Toxic Trends: Are These Subtle Delusions Controlling Your Life?* is a gripping, life-changing book that will make a difference in the way you think. I recommend it highly. Read it, digest its principles, and let the Lord change your thought patterns as your mind comes into conformity with the mind of the Master.

Mark A. Finley

INTRODUCTION

"No man is an island."

The catastrophe began with a loud roaring noise and ended with a terrible cloud of poison, pouring like a river of death over the highlands of Cameroon, Africa. The deadly cloud rose from the depths of scenic Lake Nios, famed for some of the most stunning beauty in Africa. The pristine, mountainous setting surrounding the lake masked an unseen menace. For out of the dark waters, without warning, rose a deadly channel of poison powerful enough to asphyxiate more than 1,700 people.

Pouring into nearby villages—killing countless creatures in addition to men, women, and children—the Lake Nios tragedy is a heart-rending example of nature run amok. It was beauty turned ugly—a toxic cloud in the midst of a gorgeous and apparently safe environment.

Unfortunately, the toxic tragedy that engulfed Lake Nios is being repeated near and yes, even in, your home. We are not talking about environmental toxins here. We are talking about toxic trends—a deadly circle of habits and influences flooding the world around us.

It would be difficult to live in the decade of the nineties without exposure to these toxic trends.

These toxic trends and the delusions behind them do not bring sudden death, like the deadly river of gas that poured off Lake Nios into the surrounding villages. But they are spiritually asphyxiating.

By impairing your power to think, they inhibit your ability to have clear spiritual eyesight. They can keep you from choosing right over wrong, godliness over sin, life over death.

The Cameroon Highlands surrounding Lake Nios were steeped in mysterious folklore. Tales of terror rising from the depths of its thirty-six lakes abounded. Yet there seemed to be no immediate threat or danger until that fateful day in August of 1986.

In the case of the unfortunate Cameroon Highlanders, perhaps they reasoned that "it" couldn't happen again—that nothing quite so deadly could possibly emerge from the depths of Lake Nios. Perhaps they had no other place to go. Whatever their reasons, whatever their premise for staying in the area, they were wrong.

Fatally deluded.

You, too, may have what appear to be good reasons for your current way of life. Perhaps you are living exactly the way you were raised. Or you believe none of the "borderline" things you do will have lasting effects. Or that nothing bad can happen to you.

But that's the way it is with delusions—those fascinating pieces of fiction we choose to believe. They are deceptively innocent and spiritually asphyxiating at the same time. They are often fatal—not only to the quality and quantity of life now—but throughout eternity.

To help alert you to some of the more prevalent toxic trends and the fatal delusions behind them is the purpose of this book.

"There is a way that seemeth right unto a man, but the end thereof are the ways of death" (Proverbs 14:12).

FOR THE READER

"Wham!"

I was sitting under a tree one day, deep in thought and minding my own business, when suddenly it hit me (a rock, that is).

It was 1969—the year Neil Armstrong first set foot on the moon—and I was six years old. My parents lived on a tree-lined, dead-end dirt road known as White Pine Boulevard, for reasons that soon became obvious to anyone driving down it.

There were pine needles in front of our house—lots of them. So, having made a pile of pine needles to jump in, roll in, and finally sit on, I was quite comfortably seated under a pine tree, examining (what else) a pine needle, when "it" hit me.

You see, unbeknownst to me, my two-year-old brother was engaged in his own form of exploration. Having discovered a rock about half the size of my head, he was looking for a suitable object to thump it on. It didn't take him long to catch sight of me, an unsuspecting target lost in my own little world.

It must have taken all the strength he could muster to carry "the rock," for it was a large one. But carry it he did. Indeed, he was even able to lift it quite high before letting it drop. Which brings us back to where this story began.

Other than the instant, incredible headache that followed within milliseconds of the direct hit to my cranium, my most vivid memory of this whole unfortunate tale was that I can't recall getting one whit of sympathy from my parents. At the risk of making them seem like ogres (which they aren't), I will have to reveal that my main recollection of the event (other than a temporary head injury) was being scolded for not having eyes in the back of my head!

Perhaps I will gain some sympathy now by telling this story nearly thirty years later, although that really isn't my purpose. My purpose is, instead, to make a very important point.

In publishing this book, I have a very sincere (and I believe valid) concern that some who read it will be tempted to use it like a rock. You know, to hit some unsuspecting, two-eyed, and less-than-perfect soul over the head.

Worse than that, I am afraid of the prospect that readers themselves might feel hit over the head after reading this book. So from the beginning, I would like to say that such an attack is far from what I had in mind.

Perhaps if I explain how I came to write this book, you will better understand what Madlyn and I are trying to say here. After researching and writing the book *In the Wake of Waco*, on David Koresh, I became fascinated with the power of mind control. For me, the power of mind control explained how Koresh manipulated his followers. A number of those people would have at one time been considered "cute" or "cool." They had great personalities and would have been considered least likely to join a cult.

Just for the record, some of the key elements of mind control are sleep deprivation, sensory overload, and an unbalanced diet. As I studied the mind-control methods used by cults, it became clear to me that Satan is using, in subtle ways, many of the same tactics to impair our ability to think, or make correct spiritual decisions. He is engaged in "chemical" warfare, in which the toxins are not actual chemicals, but lifestyle choices that make us less capable Christians.

To alert people to some (and by no means all) of these tactics is the purpose of this book.

I believe that a knowledge of the *reasons* why certain lifestyle choices are preferable for the Christian is the first step toward making right choices. In the Bible, God says, "My people are destroyed for lack of knowledge" (Hosea 4:6). Although many good reasons can be found in the Bible, current research also contains a wealth of evidence supporting certain lifestyle choices. Being aware of this research, as well as the biblical basis for lifestyle choices recommended in this book, can help us make better choices ourselves.

In writing this book, neither Madlyn nor myself are claiming "sainthood." I freely admit to having struggled with more than a few of the "toxic trends" outlined in these pages. Staying up into the wee hours of the night to write the sleep-deprivation chapter is one notable example of a gap between my personal conviction and occasional practice.

However, I can just as freely admit that God

has been very gracious to me, a sinner. I have much to praise Him for, especially in terms of His patience with me even when I was far from Him. And as I come to know Him more and learn more of the incredibly logical reasoning behind everything He asks me to do, many lifestyle choices have become much easier for me to make.

It is my sincere prayer that as you read this book and learn more of the "toxic trends" that truly can affect your ability to think and make right spiritual choices, you will also look beyond the trends to the Saviour who loves you, gave His life for you, and is more than willing to do abundantly above all that you ask or think. Which, by the way, means He will give you both the strength to do all that He asks you to do and an incredible sense of love and caring for your brothers and sisters in Christ who may not yet share your convictions.

CARI HAUS

When Cari and I were doing research on the book *In the Wake of Waco*, we became aware of trends that we felt definitely contributed to the fiery end of some of the people who lived at Ranch Apocalypse.

As we interviewed family members and acquaintances of the unfortunate Waco victims, we had many questions answered by some of the things we learned. For example, as we studied the significant role that heavy-metal rock music played in the lives of the Branch Davidians, we felt the desperate need for another book exposing some of the subtle trends that are entrapping hundreds and thousands of young and old today.

Thus, *Toxic Trends* was born.

Exposing toxic trends of our world serves no useful purpose unless it results in some personal action by those who choose to learn and grow from the information. I write from my heart—knowing that some of the trends we talk about are problems in my own life. And yet I am filled with courage when I think of Christ dying on that cruel cross that I might live forever in a wonderful paradise.

My prayer is that you, too, will find for yourself that abundant life so desired by people everywhere. And to those of you who have seemingly unanswerable questions and deeply rooted bad habits, might I point you to the beautiful words of Jesus, who said, "Come unto me, all ye that labour and are heavy laden, and I will give you rest" (Matthew 11:28).

MADLYN LEWIS HAMBLIN

Chapter 1

TIED TO THE TUBE

Julie Horton Banning Anderson is a gorgeous brunette with a striking figure. I met her on a sunny afternoon when I was looking for something or someone to occupy my time. During the next several years, she came to visit me regularly, so we became quite well acquainted.

Julie's troubles were matched only by the glamorous life she seemed to lead. Although she had given a baby away for adoption and had suffered through the death of one husband and divorce from another, she seemed to cope without difficulty.

As I became intimately acquainted with Julie, I started to envy her lifestyle. Beautiful and appealing, the romance in her life seemed incredibly exciting, and I secretly began thinking that perhaps my own life could be enhanced if I were liberated from work and family.

But one day, when I sat down and took inventory of my own situation, I was shocked at how much Julie was influencing me. And I suddenly realized that her sterile friendship was contributing to a downward trend in my life.

So I chose to say goodbye to Julie. But she didn't even miss me, because she was the heroine of a soap opera I had been following closely!

Without even realizing my danger, I had unwittingly believed:

DELUSION 1: WHAT I *WATCH* DOES NOT AFFECT ME!

The idea that what a person watches does not affect them is one of many promoted by Hollywood. Here is some related "fascinating fiction," which has gained broader and broader acceptance among the American public:

- TV doesn't cause violence in the world; it just reflects it.
- Violence on TV is "useful and cautionary." By suggesting that evil and harm are everywhere, television encourages us to be prepared.
- You shouldn't exercise too much caution about what your children see on television. After all, gravitating toward the forbidden is just a natural part of growing up.
- Viewers have always seen very clearly the distinction between real violence and cartoon or film violence, and their personal lives are not affected by what they view.
- Watching violence is "cathartic." A violent person might even be pacified by watching a murder.

The average American spends between twenty-three and twenty-six hours per week "tied to the tube." And the average teenager will have watched seventeen thousand hours of television before graduating from high school. In fact, more time is spent in front of a television set than at virtually any other activity besides sleeping!

Turning the TV off has never been easy, and the entertainment industry is working hard to make it even more difficult. Now you can actively play along with game shows, learn in participatory TV classrooms, and buy products on shopping channels—all from the comfort of your living room.

With the help of your remote control, you will be able to choose which news stories, sitcoms, self-help videos, and movies you want to watch and when. You will be able to read books and newspapers from around the world. E-mail will be more "in" than ever, "snail mail" will be out, and the combo TV/phone/computer you communicate with will be about the size and weight of a pad of notepaper!

TVs are acting more and more like computers, computers are becoming more and more like phones, and phones are turning into information machines. We will be living in the age of the "Super TV" with at least five hundred and possibly thousands of channels.

"This will change the world forever," said John Scully, former head of Apple Computers. "It's starting already. It's not science fiction" (*USA Today*, 18 May 1993).

If you don't like technology and don't consider yourself computer literate, not to worry. Computer wizards are working to make these new devices as easy to use as your microwave oven. The television set becomes a friendly device instead of a passive device. It will learn about you—becoming a smart agent and searching for things you want.

If you tell it you're looking for a new raincoat, it could keep an eye on all the shopping channels and save video clips of coats you might like that are on sale. Or if you like Grace Kelly movies, it could find them on the available networks and let you know the cost to order.

If the industry has its way, there won't be the haves and the have-nots. The technology will be priced and built so small schools, small businesses, and low-income people can use it, and everybody will have access to the networks.

Of course, there are good uses for much of this technology. One example of an American town that is already "wired" is Blacksburg, Virginia. In Blacksburg, you can attend and participate in a town meeting, read minutes from town council meetings, or order a building permit—all without leaving the comfort of your home. E-mail flies back and forth between town residents, and shoppers walk through the televised aisles of grocery stores, "selecting" items that will later be delivered to their doorsteps.

But there are bad uses of technology, also—as well as excessive use of otherwise good technology. One Blacksburg woman admitted that she rushes to get on-line every day—often spending as many as five hours exploring the vast world of the Internet.

The on-line offerings will soon be so vast, intriguing, and addicting, that if you are already having trouble finding the "big red switch" (that means OFF!), it isn't going to get any easier. Instead, it's going to be much, much more difficult.

There are a number of problems associated with television entertainment—in all of its forms. Here are some of them:

Problem 1: TV can easily take time from important people in our lives.

Watching TV—whether it is the news, the soaps, or "edutainment"— takes time, energy, and creativity that could otherwise be devoted to important relationships in our lives. As in the case of the soaps and Julie Horton Banning Anderson, television can be so engaging, so entertaining, so downright captivating that viewers become more attached to the screen character than to family, friends, or even God.

If this possibility seems absurd, ask yourself these questions:

- Would I go through some sort of withdrawal if I missed some favorite sporting event or television show?
- Would I go to great lengths to see or tape it or have a hard time taking my mind off it during its usual airtime—even if I'm engaged in some other activity?
- If the answers to those questions are Yes,

would I experience the same sense of loss if I missed time with my spouse or kids, church, Bible study, or prayer?

• Do I go to the same lengths to ensure that my family and spiritual priorities are met as I do to see my favorite program?

God wants a balance in our lives—and that balance involves certain priorities. Jesus said, "Thou shalt love the Lord thy God with all thy heart, and with all thy soul, and with all thy mind. This is the first and great commandment. And the second is like unto it, Thou shalt love thy neighbor as thyself" (Matthew 22:37-39).

Jesus Christ must be first, last, and best in our lives. Our love for family and friends should rank a close second. It's easy to say we believe these things, but showing that we mean them by the way we spend our time is quite another. The time we spend is an excellent index of where our true love is.

Problem 2: TV can easily distract from important tasks we should be doing.

Have you ever thought that you might be responsible for the good you might have done, if the time spent watching TV was invested in some other activity? The national average (twenty-six hours per week) is a significant piece of our lives. Over the course of a year, it amounts to 574 hours, or thirty-three days! That's a full month of time!

You could grow a pretty impressive garden, visit a lot of shut-ins, repair a tattered marriage, or learn a new and useful hobby with that many hours per year. You could open a soup kitchen for the homeless, mentor a struggling friend who looks up to you, even get a good start on a Ph.D. or at least a high-school diploma.

Could the Bible theme of right versus wrong, sin versus sinlessness, and selfishness versus selflessness carry over into television viewing too? It would seem so.

We have a choice. We can only be truly devoted to one thing. Which will it be? Entertainment of ourselves or service to others?

In the Isaiah 58 description of true religion, God says, "Is not this the fast that I have chosen? to loose the bands of wickedness, to undo the heavy burdens, and to let the oppressed go free, and that ye break every yoke? Is it not to deal thy bread to the hungry, and that thou bring the poor that are cast out to thy house? when thou seest the naked, that thou cover him; and that thou hide not thyself from thine own flesh?" (verses 6-8).

Feeding the hungry, loosing the bands of wickedness, breaking every yoke—these are time-consuming injunctions. It doesn't seem likely that we will have time to commit ourselves to these needed and very important tasks and spend much time watching television as well.

But the Bible is rather clear about our responsibilities. "Therefore to him that knoweth to do good, and doeth it not, to him it is sin" (James 4:17).

Problem 3: Difficulty reentering the real world and accepting life as it is.

The more gripping the experience, the more difficult it is to reenter the humdrum routine of our everyday life. Whether the exhilaration is from an incredible movie or forging "cyber relationships" around the planet, the result can be the same.

Mind replays are common for anyone who watches TV or goes to the movies. Six-year-old Leah Taffel saw a commercial for *Nightmare on Elm Street*. That night, she told her parents, "I can't get that scary guy out of my head" (Mark Silver, "Troubling TV Ads: Parents Who Peek at Kids TV Shows May be Shocked by Commercials" in *U.S. News & World Report*, 1 February 1993).

Nightmare on Elm Street, by the way, is the most successful horror movie to date—featuring an incinerated child molester, Freddie Krueger, who disembowels and decapitates his victims first in their dreams—then for real.

How many times have the scenes from a TV show or movie replayed in your mind? If you watch something detrimental, chances are you will see it more than once. You will see it over and over again, in your mind's eye.

Avoiding the scenes of violence and perversion is the best way to eliminate those instant replays. Solomon, who most certainly was exposed to the wide variety of entertainment that existed in his day, gave some advice that is still valid thousands of years later: "Let thine eyes look right on, and let thine eyelids look straight before thee. Ponder the path of thy feet, and let all thy ways be established. Turn not to the right hand nor to the left: remove thy foot from evil" (Proverbs 4:25-27). "Keep thy heart with all diligence; for out of it are the issues of life" (verse 23).

Problem 4: Promotes skewed sex roles, apathy toward violence, and even violent behavior.

When it comes to television, "Boys identify with violent male heroes. Girls identify with females they see being victimized," said Ron Slaby, Ph.D., a senior scientist in Newton, Massachusetts, who has studied the media's effects on children for twenty-five years. "There is a bystander effect producing an increased callousness, behavioral apathy and emotional desensitization towards violence. And finally, there is the appetite effect exhibited by some children who've viewed a great deal of glorified violence" (Mary Granfield, "Who Invited Them?" in *Family Circle*, 22 February 1994).

"Research suggests that it (TV) violence increases physical aggression in children, such as getting into fights and disrupting the play of others," writes Mortimer B. Zuckerman. "Does this increase in aggression contribute to the explosion of criminal violence? Many argue that it does. They point to studies such as one demonstrating that children who watched a lot of TV at 8 years of age have a higher propensity to commit violent crime by age 30, including the beating of their own children. (Mortimer B. Zuckerman, editorial in *U.S. News & World Report*, 2 August 1993).

More than three thousand research studies testify to the relationship between television and violence. With the exception of one, every single one of these three thousand research efforts conclude that there is a definite correlation between television viewing and violence (the one dissenting research project was paid for by NBC).

In summary, what we watch affects what we think, and what we think affects the way we act. "For as he thinketh in his heart, so is he" (Proverbs 23:7).

Jesus also said that mental participation in sin *was* a sin in itself. "Ye have heard that it was said of them of old time, Thou shalt not commit adultery: But I say unto you, That whosoever looketh on a woman to lust after her hath committed adultery with her already in his heart" (Matthew 5:27, 28).

King David, who could give a personal testimony about the results of mental participation in sin, wrote out his resolution for the rest of the world to admire and emulate: "I will set no wicked thing before mine eyes" (Psalm 101:3).

God intended for us to be changed "from glory into glory"—to more fully reflect His character as we know Him better. By "beholding" (i.e., watching) entertainment that leads away from God, we will still be changed—but not into the image God intended.

If we fill our minds with violent images—whether from television, videos, interactive television, or some other source—it will become difficult, if not impossible, to control our thoughts.

On the other hand, if we spend time with Jesus—in Bible study and prayer—our sweetest thoughts will be of Him. Christ-centered thinking, which might seem like an incredible challenge in today's "interrupt-driven" world, can, through Bible study, prayer, and purity in entertainment choices, become a much easier habit to form.

"Finally, brethren, whatsoever things are true, whatsoever things are honest, whatsoever things are just, whatsoever things are pure, whatsoever things are lovely, whatsoever things are of good report; if there be any virtue, and if there be any praise, think on these things" (Philippians 4:8)

WHAT YOU CAN DO

1. Consecrate your life to God every morning—and surrender your entertainment choices along with everything else. With His help, choose to control what goes into your mind. Be active, not reactive.

2. Budget your TV and movie time, and read ahead to find out if what you are considering watching is suitable for a Christian (i.e., asking yourself, Will this glorify God and bring me closer to Him?).

3. Use technology to control access to your TV, if you have one.
   - The Switch (about $25, call 800-535-5845) controls electricity on the set with a key. If the switch is turned off, the TV can't be turned on.
   - TimeSlot (800-653-5911), about $100, turns the set on and off at certain times and keeps track of the amount of time it is used.

4. Before turning on the TV, ask yourself these questions:

- Does the show I plan to watch promote Christian values?
- Will this program bring out the best in me, making me a better person?
- Will the commercials shown during breaks in the programming have a positive spiritual impact on my life?
- Is this the best way for me to spend my recreational time?
- Are the characters I am watching and the scenes they portray honorable and virtuous?
- Will the Bible and my everyday life still seem interesting after I finish viewing this program?

5. If you have tried all of these options and still have trouble controlling your television set, you can always "get radical" and just get rid of it!

FINAL THOUGHT

"Ye shall know the truth, and the truth shall make you free" (John 8:32).

Chapter 2

THE ELECTRONIC ESCAPE

John Greene* rocks back in his posh leather chair, eyes closed and brow knit in deep concentration. A corporate CEO by day, Greene owns and operates a construction company. Working long hours, he often jets overseas in pursuit of lucrative contracts. But now—just now—John Greene's mind is drifting far away from megadeals and multimillion-dollar skyrises. For during his "off time," in the middle of the night, John Greene is a serial killer.

And the subject that thoroughly arrests his attention so often is not how to manage his company, but the manner of death for his latest victim.

"So what will it be?" John turns to his wife, Sara, who is leaning over his shoulder. "Electrocution, strangling, open-heart surgery, or a combination of the above?" At his last suggestion, John lets out a low, throaty laugh.

"You should be behind bars." Sara gives him a callous wink before turning back to check on the children. John is an expert at inflicting nightmarish cruelty—and Sara knows it. For the types of crimes he regularly commits, more than one man has faced a firing squad, or at the very least, rotted in jail for the rest of his life.

As a matter of fact, there is only one reason why John Greene isn't behind bars. The crime scenes he relishes are committed without ever breaking the law. That's why tonight, John sits, not behind bars, but in front of his computer screen—perpetrating the violence he craves so desperately.

An apparently good citizen, prosperous businessman, and doting father by day, John lets out his aggressions by night with the aid of his personal computer and violent video games. John Greene has unwittingly fallen for:

FATAL DELUSION 2: WHAT I EXPERIENCE DOES NOT AFFECT ME.

In other words, I can do whatever I wish in a computer or video game, and since it is only a game—it is not wrong. Below is some other "fascinating fiction" commonly believed about video and computer games:

- People (kids included) know the difference between video-game action and on-the-street, in-your-face action. Turning the computer on and off—with your own power—somehow separates the game from reality.
- Video games are an innocent form of entertainment. Even when players engage in

violence or other immoral behavior, it has no lasting effect on their personal character.

- If you had a bad day, it's better to take out your aggressions in video games than in real life, even if that means "ripping a couple of heads off."

Video games are an increasingly popular form of entertainment in America today. Sales of video games rake in $5.3 billion a year in revenue alone. It's estimated that Sega or Nintendo game sets are in more than fifty million American homes. And American kids with a video game in their home play an average of one-and-a-half hours on the video game per day (in addition to whatever TV they may watch). Clearly, John Greene is not alone in his obsession.

"The kids get it right away," wrote Philip Elmer-Dewitt in a recent issue of *Time* magazine. "Nobody has to explain to a ten-year-old boy what's so great about video games. Just sit him down in front of a Sega Genesis or Super Nintendo machine, shove a cartridge into the slot and he's gone—body, mind and soul—into a make-believe world that's better than sleep, better than supper and a heck of a lot better than school."

TV is a solitary, physically nonparticipatory experience that threatens to turn kids into couch potatoes or zombies. Video games go one step farther than television. They get the couch potato off the couch—and physically involved in what's on the screen. They are just one use for "interactive television."

Interactive, one of the latest high-tech

buzzwords, can mean anything from making your own music videos to ordering pizza through your TV set. The essence of it is that you are an active participant. Instead of watching a movie, you direct a character's actions. Instead of turning a book's pages, you direct the computer to find the most relevant passages. Multimedia—often mentioned hand in hand with interactive entertainment—combines pictures, sound, video, animation, and text. Interactive programs can be transmitted to phones, TV sets, and computers by fiber-optic cables and data "superhighways."

But video games and interactive television are just the beginning of what's coming down the pike in terms of computer entertainment. The hottest computer sensory games will take advantage of "virtual reality," which will allow players to "see and experience places and events as though they were actually there."

Imagine putting on a helmet and gloves and, wired to a computer, actually experiencing a walk on Mars. Or revisiting a childhood experience without leaving your living room. Or cooking in a dream kitchen that hasn't been built. Just when you thought ordinary reality was hard enough to comprehend, Hollywood is perfecting virtual reality. Also known as VR, this emerging technology will allow people wearing high-tech gadgetry to enter and interact with computer-generated worlds.

Through virtual reality, you can create a three-dimensional world. By using special eyewear and motion-sensitive gloves, or full body suits, you can control the action on the screen.

The publishing houses of Manhattan, authors, directors, writers, and musicians see interactive media as a vast new blank canvas on which to paint.

"There are some directors in Hollywood who are absolutely fascinated by the whole idea of interactivity," says Brian Fargo, president of interactive game maker Interplay Productions.

Virtually every major studio in Hollywood has set up a subsidiary to create interactive products.

Typically, these interactive projects are computer adventure games based on blockbuster movies.

Virtual reality has already arrived for millions of participants at amusement parks and arcades. A top draw at one park: the Cybergate space-battle team game. Up to six players sit in Hovercraft-like pods; 3-D headsets with wrap-around screens and earphones immerse them in the feeling of space travel.

Or you can step into an elevator at the new pyramid-shaped Luxor Las Vegas casino/hotel and feel like you've just fallen eight thousand feet. The "experience" is simulated by presenting a film that moves in motion with the elevator room. It's all an illusion.Whether you call it a simulator, a movie ride, or virtual-reality movie, it's you-are-there-without-really-being-there entertainment.

In another *Back to the Future* trip, you sit in a car seat before a giant screen—riding through time, crossing paths with prehistoric dinosaurs, plummeting down volcanic tunnels, and cascading over glacial ice fields.

There are many good uses for virtual reality. Pilot training, architectural design, and presurgery practice sessions are just a few of the many possibilities being pursued. But other applications, such as "cyborgasm" and "cybersex," which are reportedly "heavy on moaning," sound a little less than uplifting. "We may be becoming a nation of New Victorians," wrote one enthusiastic virtual-reality reviewer. "Virginity is being revalued. Celibacy is more common, even among dating twentysomethings. And monogamy sounds pretty good, even to bed 'n' bored baby boomers. . . . Safe sex today doesn't require a partner. Just imagination and maybe a TV, a phone or a VCR. . . . We have seen the future of sex, and it is computerized" (Elizabeth Snead, "Subbing for Sex: More Remote Sources of Satisfaction" in *USA Today*, 26 November 1991).

"Cybersex" advocates tout "long-distance sex" as an effective way to fight the AIDS epidemic. However, despite whatever mitigating effect "cybersex" might have on AIDS or venereal disease, it seems there are other, preferable methods for combating such illnesses. Many Christians may easily see a problem with "cybersex," but what about the many apparently innocent video games on the market today?

What's wrong with playing video games?

Video games have not been around as long as television, so a wealth of studies have not yet been performed. However, some of the problems that have already surfaced are similar to those discussed in the television chapter. Even the most innocent-seeming games can become an obsession—leading to wasted time, damaged family relationships, or poor spending choices. And because of the interactive nature of virtual reality and video games, it would seem that they may be even more gripping and therefore more powerful than television.

The reaction to stressful (though exciting) entertainment can have a physical as well as an emotional effect on our bodies. In one documented case, "an EKG monitoring system was placed on a man with known heart disease while he was watching the Boston Celtics, his favorite team in the playoffs. From the late morning until midafternoon, just before the game started, his heart rate ranged from 60 to 80 beats per minute. But then when the game started at 4:00 p.m., his heart rate began to vary from 80 to 120, and he was showing increasing 'irritability' or irregularities in his heart rate.

"During the next hours, as the game got more exciting, his heart rate increased to 150 beats per minute, and in conjunction with the high heart rate, there were multiple episodes of heart irregularities. If they had been persistent, these irregularities could have been fatal. It wasn't until two hours after the game that his heart rate returned to normal and the irregularities disappeared" (Kenneth Cooper, *The Aerobics Program for Total Well-being*, 190, 191).

The above example was from watching television—which though emotionally exciting is still basically a couch-potato activity. Video games, which require some degree of physical exertion as well and can be all the more gripping, have actually sent a number of children into convulsions. Some videogame producers have actually issued warnings and disclaimers on the outsides of video-game sets.

As video games become more and more like real-life experiences, it will become increasingly difficult to adjust to reality. After all, why take the time to work through problems with relationships or give whole-hearted effort to some challenging but potentially rewarding task, when you can escape it all into a controllable computerized world?

"Some 80 percent of Americans feel that TV violence is harmful to our society and that there is too much of it in our entertainment," writes Mortimer B. Zuckerman (Mortimer B. Zuckerman, editorial in *U.S. News & World Report*, 2 August 1993). Would not the same social problems that have surfaced as a result of TV violence, also be connected with video game violence? It's not always easy to separate the effects of video/computer games from movies, but the evidence is beginning to accumulate. There are a number of Bible principles that would apply to virtual reality and video games. They include:

Principle #1: We cannot keep our eye single to the glory of God and be a split personality at the same time.

The "split personality" of a doting parent, responsible citizen, and good Christian person who transforms into a murderous fiend with the flip of the big red switch, then somehow leaves behind all the emotional baggage accumulated from near-death experiences and other emotionally compelling situations just doesn't fit. "Doth a fountain send forth at the same place sweet water and bitter? Can the fig tree, my brethren, bear olive berries? either a vine, figs? so can no fountain both yield salt water and fresh" (James 3:11, 12).

The Bible makes it clear that there is a difference between peace-loving Christians and those who enjoy strife, envying, and every evil work (a fitting description for some violent video games). "If ye have bitter envying and strife in your hearts, glory not, and lie not against the truth. This wisdom descendeth not from above, but is earthly, sensual, devilish. For where envying and strife is, there is confusion and every evil work. But the wisdom that is from above is first pure, then peaceable, gentle, and easy to be intreated, full of mercy and good fruits, without partiality, and without hypocrisy. And the fruit of righteousness is sown in peace of them that make peace" (James 3:14-18).

We are forming habits here—habits that will be with us for the rest of our lives and, if we are saved, throughout eternity. While we can change our habits through the grace of God, how much easier to form the habit of being kind, thoughtful, and commandment keeping in the first place—in both our work and our play. "Can the

Ethiopian change his skin, or the leopard his spots? then may ye also do good, that are accustomed to do evil" (Jeremiah 13:23).

Principle 2: God is love, and we are to be like Him.

The principle of love for our fellow humans is repeated throughout the Bible and embodied in the golden rule of Matthew 7: "All things whatsoever ye would that men should do to you, do ye even so to them: for this is the law and the prophets" (verse 12).

Video games that promote decidedly unkind acts tear down, rather than build up, our love and empathy for other human beings. One can hardly imagine the God who died for us playing games featuring the torture and mutilation of His creation—whether animal or human.

The same is true for the committed Christian, who by the grace of God is becoming more and more like Jesus. "He that saith he is in the light, and hateth his brother, is in darkness even until now. He that loveth his brother abideth in the light, and there is none occasion of stumbling in him. But he that hateth his brother is in darkness, and walketh in darkness, and knoweth not whither he goeth, because that darkness hath blinded his eyes" (1 John 2:9-11).

Principle 3: True pleasure and happiness come only through Christ.

True peace and lasting pleasure come only from Christ. God has promised to give those who love Him an abiding peace even in difficult times and an eternity of joy in heaven. But if our main source of pleasure is video games—whether they be entertainment or "edutainment"—it will be impossible to remain focused on Christ at the same time. Jesus said, "No man can serve two masters: for either he will hate the one, and love the other; or else he will hold to the one, and despise the other" (Matthew 6:24).

If we choose Christ as our Lord and Master, He has promised us great things. "You will show me the path of life. In Your presence is fullness of joy; at Your right hand are pleasures forevermore" (Psalm 16:1, NKJV). "Delight thyself also in the Lord; and he shall give thee the desires of thine heart" (Psalm 37:4). "If thou turn away thy foot from the sabbath, from doing thy pleasure on my holy day; and call the sabbath a delight, the holy of the Lord, honourable; and shalt honour him, not doing thine own ways, nor finding thine own pleasure, nor speaking thine own words: Then shalt thou delight thyself in the Lord; and I will cause thee to ride upon the high places of the earth, and feed thee with the heritage of Jacob thy father: for the mouth of the Lord hath spoken it" (Isaiah 58:13, 14).

It's true that there is self-denial involved in the Christian walk. Perhaps all of your friends are playing video games, or you find them especially enjoyable. But if you are playing games that are detrimental to your Christian growth or time with Jesus, Jesus invites you to "take up your cross and follow me."

THE ELECTRONIC ESCAPE

Moses, as a young man, had to make choices between the lifestyle before him at Pharoah's palace, and what he knew to be right. "By faith Moses, when he was come to years refused to be called the son of Pharoah's daughter; choosing rather to suffer affliction with the people of God, than to enjoy the pleasures of sin for a season" (Hebrews 11:24, 25).

Heaven is worth any sacrifice—even a most enjoyable form of entertainment. "The kingdom of heaven is like unto a merchant man, seeking goodly pearls: who, when he had found one pearl of great price, went and sold all that he had, and bought it" (Matthew 13:45, 46).

WHAT YOU CAN DO

If you have questions about video games you like to play, or virtual reality, you might answer those questions through a study of recreation versus amusement:

- Recreation should re-create, strengthen, and build up. It should refresh your mind and body and enable you to return with new vigor to your daily activities.
- Amusement is engaged in for the sole purpose of pleasure. It is often carried to excess. It absorbs the energies that are required for useful work and proves a hindrance to success.

Then ask yourself these questions:

- Does the form of entertainment I am considering lead to obsessive behavior on my part?

- Would this game make me uninterested in secret prayer, Bible study, and devotion?
- Does this game encourage pride, selfishness, or unholy thoughts or actions?
- Is acting out sin a part of the game—such as theft, adultery, murder, or covetousness?
- If this game includes acting out an activity that in real life would definitely be sinful, is it deadening my sensibilities to that sin?
- Does this game make me a better person, or at the very least, not make me a less loving and compassionate person?

Even an apparently harmless video game can become addictive. If you think a certain form of entertainment may be harmful, but for some reason don't feel sure, consider giving it up for a specified period of time just to see what effect that has on your life. If you can't even imagine going without a video game for three days to a week, chances are you are addicted and will need to take steps to reduce the importance of that game to your life.

*name changed

Chapter 3

THE DiGiTAL DECADE

It's showtime in Bucharest, Romania and the performer gyrating across the stage is none other than the legendary Michael Jackson. Thousands of Rumanians—relishing their newfound freedom from communism—flock to the concert (Wayne Robins, "They Swooned in Romania" in *New York Newsday*, 12 October 1992).

The music has just begun, and the fans are already swaying and twisting to the beat. Their bodily contortions grow wilder as the music of Jackson's highly amplified band pulsates through the concert hall. Some concert-goers seem dazed. Others look hypnotized. Caught in a high state of exhilaration, they temporarily abandon any self-restraint and clamor for more potent doses of the druglike music. Then, in the middle of the concert, video cameras pick up something unusual. Televised pictures of unconscious persons being passed overhead to a waiting medical staff for resuscitation flash across the screen. What type of music is this—powerful enough to hypnotize, send into a frenzy, or render unconscious those who listen to it? Could these Romanians have been seduced by the age-old notion:

DELUSION 3: I AM NOT AFFECTED BY WHAT I HEAR.

As always, some fascinating fiction accompanies the delusion:

- I listen to the music, not the objectionable lyrics, so the music has no negative effect on me.
- I listen to Christian rock, and the lyrics are not objectionable, so neither is the music.
- I like "so-and-so's" music, and the fact that she/he lives a lifestyle that is obviously far from God's plan should have no effect on my choice.

Music ranks second only to television in the influence it wields over the values of children. The average teenager listens to 10,500 hours of music (no, not Handel's *Messiah*) between the seventh and twelfth grades. Singers and musicians are the heroes, the idols that young people want to emulate. Yet many popular songs focus on themes of sex, Satanism, drugs, or violence.

Popular groups today sing about women being raped, hatred toward police officers, and racial violence—often performing degrading acts onstage. Those who feel they can listen to the music of their choice and not be affected are missing out on a well-known fact that has been known for literally thousands of years:

Music is an extremely powerful form of communication.

The ancient philosopher Aristotle was aware of the power of music. More than three centuries before Christ, he wrote that "rhythm and melody can 'bring about a change in the soul of the listener'" (Paul Hamel, *The Christian and His Music* [Hagerstown, Md.: Review and Herald, 1973], 31).

Hysterical crowds are not limited to rock-music concerts. History records incidents of crowds losing control at various concerts over the centuries. "Music is a curiously subtle art with innumerable, varying emotional connotations. It is made up of many ingredients and, according to the proportions of these components, it can be soothing or invigorating, ennobling or vulgarizing. It has power for evil as well as for good," wrote Howard Hanson, a prominent composer formerly with the Eastern School of Music (*American Journal of Psychiatry*, 99:317).

But what makes music so powerful?

Part of the power is in the rhythm, for we ourselves are creatures of rhythm.

"There is rhythm in respiration, heartbeat, speech, gait, etc. The cerebral hemisphere are in a perpetual state of swing day and night" (*American Mercury*, September 1961, 46). Rhythm is also a natural part of music—and the rhythm of music is either in harmony with nature or out of step with our natural rhythms. And the music is either uplifting or degrading. There are some intrinsic problems with the rhythm of much of the popular music today. In research studies in which plants were played rock music, they did their utmost to reach away from the sound. In another documented case, a teenage girl began to have dangerous heart rhythms during surgery. She just happened to be listening to contemporary Christian music on her headphones during the surgery. When the doctors removed the headphones, her heart returned to normal function!

Recent studies of music and its effects on surgery patients have demonstrated that music has a positive effect on pain control before, during, and after surgery. Anesthetized patients who undergo surgery during music require less medication for pain. Music played during surgery has even been credited with improving the efficiency of the surgeons themselves! "Without music, life would be a mistake," Nietzsche wrote in 1889. An article in the *Journal of the American Medical Association* put a new twist on Nietzsche's statement: "Our data prompt us to ponder if, without music, surgery would be a mistake" (*JAMA*, 21 September 1994, 272:11). "Music is much of the stuff which is in and of itself the most powerful stimulant known among the perceptual processes. . . . Music operates on our emotional faculty with greater intensiveness and rapidity than the product of almost any other act," wrote Dr. Schoen in *The Psychology of Music* (Max Shoen, 1988, Report Services, 39).

Thanks to technology, music today is more powerful than ever.

With the widespread application of computers in the creation and recording of music, musical performance has become a big computer game, less dependent than ever on the human quality of a voice or musical craftsmanship. Computer expertise made chart toppers out of performers who couldn't sing, write, or play—as in the case of Grammy winners Milli Vanilli.

Electronic musicians have the ability to experiment over and over again until they get just the right "effect," which is more often than not some sort of major impact on the listener.

So what's wrong with listening to certain types of music?

Here are a few of the problems that have emerged with music that has proven less than beneficial to its listeners:

• Negative effects on teenage behavior.

In a recent study, teenagers who preferred heavy metal and rap music were compared with those who preferred other types of music. Results indicated that adolescents who preferred heavy metal and rap had a higher incidence of below-average school grades, school behavior problems, sexual activity, drug and alcohol use, and arrests (*Adolescence*, 29:115, Fall 1994).

• Excessive amplification causes hearing loss.

Three decades after the rock revolution, more and more performers are discovering that their hearing is permanently impaired. "In order to protect themselves from their own music," writes Paul Hamel, "many rock musicians have started using earplugs" (Paul Hamel, *The Christian and His Music* [Hagerstown, Md.: Review and Herald Pub. Assn., 1973], 146, 147).

• Sensory overload.

Where can you go today and *not* be bombarded with music? From grocery stores to funeral parlors, the music is on and playing constantly. The invention of the Walkman made listening to music possible while exercising, and now you can even listen to a radio while swimming with "Aqua Tunes," a lightweight, waterproof pouch and earplug that let a swimmer listen to the radio or cassette player while doing laps. Music is beautiful—but good music demands to be listened to—not played in the background twenty-four hours a day.

• Music circumvents the decision portion of your brain

When people listen to the radio nonstop, they are putting themselves in the hands of the disc jockeys and musicians who are providing the music. And when the music is not wholesome or uplifting, it reaches people's brains anyway.

So what does the Bible say about music?

If there were a verse saying, "Thou shalt not listen to rock, rap, jazz, classical, or some other specified list of objectionable music," it would certainly have been most convenient, as well as often quoted. Music certainly played an important role in a number of Bible stories. Music was:

- sung by Miriam and the Israelites after crossing the Red Sea.
- an integral part of the sanctuary worship service.
- a soother for the melancholy of Saul.
- a joy and source of inspiration to King David.
- taught in the schools of the prophets.
- a signal for the three worthies and others on the plain of Dura to bow to the golden image.
- refused by King Darius while Daniel was in the lion's den.
- performed by an angelic choir at the birth of Christ.
- heard during John the revelator's vision of heaven.

Music also accompanied instances of sin, such as:

- the seduction of Israelite men by the Moabitish women.
- the worship of the golden calf below Mt. Sinai.
- religious feasts of the Philistines.

Music no doubt played an integral part at the idolatrous feast of Belshazzar and other heathen festivals as well. Given the power of music, it seems safe to assume that there was a vast difference between the music at a Philistine religious festival and the songs sung at the dedication of Solomon's temple.

So the Bible gives us examples of two types of music—that which uplifted and that which destroyed. It is up to us to determine which music today has the power for good.

WHAT YOU CAN DO

Every now and then, it's a good idea to evaluate the music you are listening to. Even if you feel your choice of music is above reproach, you might still be exposed to objectionable music at times or feel a need to make some changes. Pray sincerely for guidance, and be willing to accept whatever truths you learn. As Christians, it's important for us to examine carefully every influence in our lives—including music. That's what Paul was talking about in 1 Thessalonians 5:21, when he wrote, "Prove all things; hold fast that which is good." Ask yourself these questions about your favorite music:

· Does it bring me closer to Jesus?
· Are the lyrics pure and holy, or at the very least, inoffensive? Or do they promote violence, adultery, or some other sin?
· Is the music such that it is receiving the personal imprint of a particular musician and his or her lifestyle? If so, is their lifestyle godly?
· If I believe the music I am currently listening to seems inappropriate for a Christian, are there other forms of music that I might develop an appreciation for and enjoy just as much?

If after prayer and careful consideration, you

come to the conclusion that the music you have listened to is sinful, it's important to confess your sin and ask God's forgiveness. "He that covereth his sins shall not prosper: but whoso confesseth and forsaketh them shall have mercy" (Proverbs 28:13).

The next step is to cleanse your home of any objectionable music, following the advice of Paul, who realized how easy it is for us to fall back into our old habits: Make not provision for the flesh, to fulfil the lusts thereof" (Romans 13:14).

Having done these things, we can say with Paul again, "Thanks be to God, which giveth us the victory through our Lord Jesus Christ" (1 Corinthians 15:57).

FINAL THOUGHT

As the wind can rise from a gentle breeze to a raging hurricane, so music can enchant or destroy us.

Chapter 4

YOU *ARE* WHAT YOU READ

Alan Brown* bent over his high-school science test, his face troubled, deep in thought. He had answered every question on the exam except for one—and he was stumped. "Does the earth revolve around the sun, or does the sun circle the earth?" That was the question of the hour. Finally, Alan sighed, circled the wrong answer, and handed in his test.

If you, like Alan, did not know what revolves around what in our solar system, not to worry! You are not alone. In a recent poll, 21 percent of Americans got the wrong answer to this simple question of science, and another 7 percent didn't know!

Maybe that has something to do with the low math and science scores of U.S. students, as reported in a 1993 study by *Science News*. The study found that U.S. students on both the elementary and secondary levels lag significantly behind their Asian counterparts when it comes to math and science ("U. S. Complacency Adds to Math Woes," *Science News*, 9 January 1993).

You Are What You Read

All these last-or-near-last-place finishes might sound incredibly dismal—but the American students did place first in one category. They watched more TV than any of their counterparts! What is happening to us? Americans *do* read, for when a current poll asked a group of Americans what they were currently reading, 25 percent of them cited mystery/thrillers and 1 percent romance novels or "bodice rippers." Only 6 percent said they read the Bible or other religious books (Marcy E. Mullins, "USA Snapshots: What People Are Reading," *USA Today*, 9 March 1993). Maybe the problem isn't so much that we don't read, but *what* we read. Maybe we have fallen unwittingly into the trap of:

Delusion 4: I am not affected by what I read.

As with every delusion, there is some fascinating fiction that accompanies this trend:

- How much or how well I read has nothing to do with my success in life.
- TV offers much of the same information I would find in books. I prefer to watch TV, so it's not necessary for me to read.

As a nation, we seem to be caught up in a full-scale slide some have dubbed "the dumbing of America." Reading used to be considered the fountain of knowledge, the prerequisite for success, the key to a new and more prosperous world. The American founding fathers were literate and well-read. The American colonies, during the 1700s, boasted a higher literacy rate than even

England itself!

Just before the Revolutionary War, General Gage reported to the British government that all the men in the colonies were "lawyers, and smatterers in law." They would have had to be to understand the intellectually oriented sermons by the likes of Jonathan Edwards. And so would have their descendents who listened to lengthy debates by such men as Abraham Lincoln and Stephen Douglas.

These men did not cater to intellectual babes. Their sentences were long and incredibly structured, requiring careful listening. Once when Lincoln and Douglas met for a debate, they ran "slightly over" the appointed time to quit. Douglas started it—by speaking for a mere two hours extra. Whereupon he graciously suggested that his audience take a quick meal break and return to hear his opponent. By the time Abraham Lincoln had finished his oratory, their listeners had heard more than seven hours of detailed, proselike debate.

And as history records, Lincoln, Douglas, and other politicians literally traveled the country speaking to crowds in this manner. It had to be a literate America. With the advent of the silver screen, however, books began to lose their hold over public discourse. Although political campaigns and advertising still speak through the print media, television has transformed many of the messages we hear.

Television speaks through a series of often-disjointed images. Shifting scenes rapidly to hold their viewing audience, newscasters slip from topic to topic, connecting them only with a "now this" or similar proclamation. As a matter of fact, the average television scene is only three-and-a-half seconds long.

Television is entertainment oriented. Reading can be entertaining, but it is more information oriented. Think about it. Why do news anchors drop everything and rush to the latest national disaster, often arriving on the very day it happens? At one time, people heard mostly the news that was relevant to their everyday life. But with the advent of television, the Gulf War; the burning of the Branch Davidians' complex in Waco, Texas; the Oklahoma bombing; and the O. J. Simpson trial can be dropped right into our living rooms.

For many, seeing these images on the screen translates into believing, and more than believing. That's what makes television so powerful. Images. Like the starving children of Somalia flickering across the screen. Or the unfortunate German skier who slammed into a metal post during a pre-Olympic race and died before the eyes of the world—over and over again. Or the dead American soldier being dragged through the streets of Somalia.

These scenes will be etched in memory—at least for some of us—as long as we live on this earth. Images are powerful. That's why some go so far as to speculate that this is the reason God included the second commandment in the Decalogue: "Thou shalt not make . . . any graven image." Could it be that persons so used to seeing concrete, physical evidence of everything they are told will have trouble connecting with an abstract deity—a God—who wants to be a part of their lives, yet whom they cannot physically see?

At one time, futurists predicted the appearance of a "Big Brother" who would take away our freedoms, thinking for us and not allowing us the privilege of reading what we want. That type of force may no longer be necessary. People are so awash in a sea of information that they're drowning in irrelevance. It's easier to be entertained than enlightened, to let someone else think for us than to think for ourselves. Once out of school, nearly 60 percent of all adult Americans never read a single book, preferring, instead, to spend their leisure time watching television.

Others who do read books may be doing it for the wrong reasons—according to author David Blum in *New York Magazine.* "Over the past two years, several serious books with weighty, intellectual themes have reached the best-seller list," Blum wrote, but "experts believe the books are not being read, they are simply being bought for 'snob' appeal" ("Couch Potatoes" [reprint from 20 July 1987] 19 April 1993, 26:56+).

Books may be entertaining, but they can be so much more than that. "Every great man owes a good share of his greatness to the legacy of books handed down to him by preceding generations. Of all the multiplied opportunities our modern era offers young persons, the most precious is the opportunity to own and read good books," wrote John Snyder.

His comments reflected the sentiments of many Americans just a century ago. Why were books—good books—deemed so valuable? "Our ancestors made a good many mistakes for us, and we do not need to make them over again unless we want to," Snyder wrote. "Whoever is truly growing in taste and culture must feel an ever-increasing appreciation of the value, the charm, and the power of good books" (John Snyder, *I Love Books* [Hagerstown, Md.: Review and Herald, 1951]).

"Except a living man," wrote Charles Kingsley, "there is nothing more wonderful than a book—a message from the dead—from human souls whom we never saw, who lived, perhaps, thousands of miles away, and yet these, on little sheets of paper, speak to us, amuse, vivify us, teach us, comfort us, open their hearts to us as brothers" (ibid., 26).

Thanks to desktop publishing, multi-media, quick-print machines, and glorified copiers, it has never been easier for writers to get their works into some form of print. And therein may lay just one more challenge—the information glut. A ten-year-old boy wrote a famous review of a nineteenth-century book about owls:. "This book," he said, "tells more about owls than I want to know."

Today's challenge for us is not just to read, but to read the books and literature that will give us the most benefit. There are some biblical principles that apply to our reading habits. Throughout the Bible, but especially in the book of Proverbs, the pursuit of knowledge is encouraged. "To know wisdom and instruction; to perceive the words of understanding; to receive the instruction of wisdom, justice, and judgment, and equity; to give subtilty to the simple, to the young man knowledge and discretion. A wise man will hear, and will increase learning; and a man of understanding shall attain unto wise counsels"(Proverbs 1:2-5).

One of the best sources of knowledge is thought-provoking books, not the least of which should be the Bible itself. In the Bible, we not only learn many things about how best to live our lives—but we learn that God Himself is the fountain of all knowledge. "The fear of the Lord is the beginning of wisdom" (Proverbs 9:10). Through the Bible, God encourages us to purity of thought and action. "Finally, brethren, whatsoever things are true, whatsoever things are honest, whatsoever things are just, whatsoever things are pure, whatsoever things are lovely, whatsoever things are of good report; if there be any virtue, and if there be any praise, think on these things" (Philippians 4:8).

It is difficult to feast one's mind on romance novels, even Christian ones (dubbed by one author as "sanitary syrup"), then keep the thoughts centered on Christ. Exciting stories—whether on television, played out in video games, or read in a book—frequently lead to daydreaming and an inability to cope with life as it really is.

Harold Shryock, M.D., has some interesting comments on daydreaming in his book *Your Amazing Body*.

> The content of your daydreams indexes your character. If you want to determine the quality of your character, you do not have to take tests or fill out complicated question-

naires. Simply recall your last few "air castles," and notice whether they were selfish or unselfish, vulgar or pure, cowardly or courageous, pessimistic or optimistic, full of doubts or full of courage.

Unhappy people have a special tendency to overindulge their imaginations. When actual life is not pleasant, the person who feels thwarted easily builds mental pictures of the way he wishes life could be. In this kind of daydreaming, the disappointed person is always the hero. In his daydreams he accomplishes great things—things he cannot accomplish in reality. Such a person derives his pleasures and satisfactions more from his daydreams than from the things he carries forward in real life. Such an unhealthy situation robs the individual of the zest and determination necessary to overcome obstacles and to succeed in spite of hardships (125, 126).

It's only natural to think about what we read. But any type of reading that inspires impure, unkind, or self-centered thinking is detrimental to our Christian experience. It's important that we as Christians, then, consider carefully what we are going to read and select those books and magazines that encourage us in our walk with Christ.

You are what you read.

What can you as an individual do in this "information age" to select the best reading matter and deal with the torrents of information available to you today? Here are some ideas:

- If you are already a reader, reconsider what you are reading. Is it entertainment or enlightenment? Is it simply keeping you occupied or making you a better person? Are the values in your reading material consistent with your own spiritual values?

- If you are not a reader (but just happened to read this book!)—consider making reading a larger part of your life. Look for books that will have a positive impact on your life and challenge your mind. (The Bible is a good place to start!)

- If you have children, encourage them to read. Ben Carson, the well-known surgeon, credits much of his success to his mother's requirement that he read a certain amount each week. You can help your children form a lifelong habit that will benefit them in school.

- When tempted to turn on the tube or launch into a less-than-worthy book, consider these bits of wisdom about reading:

- "A man's mind is known by the company it keeps." (That goes for women too!) *James Russell Lowell* (ibid., 64). John Snyder, *I Love Books*

- Without a love for books the richest man is poor. *Anonymous* (ibid., 94).

- Reading is the heart and soul of culture in its highest form. *Walter B. Pitkin* (ibid., 117).

---

*Not his real name.

Chapter 5

LiFE iN THE TWiLiGHT ZONE

At one time, Dave Truitt was his company's "golden boy." A loving father, he taught his two girls to fly-fish. A devoted husband, his marriage to his childhood sweetheart was as firmly rooted as the trees that shade his country home. But that was then.

This is now. Today, Dave Truitt is only a shadow of the man he used to be. He is unable to work, unable to feel emotions like love, and panics over even simple decisions like choosing a coffee mug. He asks his wife, Kathy, the same questions over and over again, because he can't remember the answers. Dave Truitt snaps at his daughters, then turns to Kathy and makes comments like, "I know I'm supposed to love you, and I know I did once, but I just don't feel anything."

"Nothing excites him," says Kathy. "Nothing is fun."[1]

What happened to this hard-working, loving father and husband from Toledo, Washington? What tragic twist turned a contented country man into a person devoid of memory, love, and virtually any other emotion?

It started with a heroic effort for his company. In a pinch, his employer needed him badly. So he worked thirty hours straight. It ended with Dave Truitt asleep at the wheel, his Ford Bronco twisted around a telephone pole and Dave himself in a coma for more than six weeks. For Dave Truitt was also suffering from:

DELUSION 5: IT DOES NOT MATTER HOW MUCH SLEEP I MISS.

As with the other delusions discussed in this book, there is some "fascinating fiction" involved here too:

- If I do fall behind on sleep, I can catch up on the weekends.
- I would never fall asleep at the wheel, since I would sense my condition and stop the car. (It only takes five seconds.)
- I require considerably less sleep than the rest of the human race. (Not true for very many people.)
- I'm young and energetic. I can get by on less sleep.

Unfortunately, millions of Americans are chronically sleep deprived, trying to get by on six hours or even less. In many households, cheating on sleep has become an unconscious and harmful habit.

"In its mild form, it's watching Ted Koppel and going to bed late and then getting up early to go to the gym," declares Dr. Charles Pollak, head of the sleep-disorder center at Cornell University.[2] In extreme cases, people stay up most of the night, seeing how little sleep will keep them going. They try to compensate by snoozing late on weekends, but that makes up for only part of the shortfall. Both cultural and economic forces are combining to turn the U.S. into a twenty-four-hour society. We live in a society where mothers work outside the home; stores don't close; assembly lines never stop. TV and radio stations "rock around the clock." Business executives feel compelled, by their interest in global markets, to blearily check the foreign stock exchange in the middle of the night.

So what's wrong with missing sleep on a regular basis?

Plenty! Sleep loss:

1. Interferes with the ability to learn.

   Teachers say they are confronting more and more draggy pupils even in elementary school. Sleepy youngsters are arriving late to class, forgetting assignments, moving at a snail's pace from task to task, and sometimes dropping their heads on their desks to catch a few winks.

   Fifteen to 20 percent of high-school students admit to falling asleep during class at least once a week, says Mary Carskadon of Brown University. College students are notorious for nodding off in class and hibernating on weekends. Phil Simon, a twenty-year-old junior at the University of Oregon in Eugene, is not unusual. During the week, he rises anytime between 7:30 a.m. and 11:00

a.m., depending on his classes, and retires some-times between 1:00 a.m. and 2:30 a.m. He naps whenever he gets a chance, but that does not al-ways work well. "A few weeks ago," he recalls, "I had a break between two morning classes, so I slept. But when I woke up, the morning class I had attended felt like it never happened. It seemed more like a dream." On weekends he heads for bed at 3:00 a.m. and doesn't get up until 1:00 p.m. (Anastasia Toufexis, "Drowsy America" in *Time*, 17 December, 1990).

2. Makes people irritable.

One of the most insidious consequences of skimping on sleep is the irritability that in-creasingly pervades society. Weariness corrodes civility and erases humor, traits that often can ease everyday frustrations. Without sufficient sleep, tempers flare faster and hot-ter at the slightest offense.

3. Increases on-the-job mistakes and accidents.

Research estimates show:

   - At least 200,000 traffic accidents annually involve driver fatigue.
   - One-third of fatal truck accidents are directly connected to loss of sleep.
   - 100,000 accidental deaths a year are due to work-related fatigue.
   - Sixteen billion dollars are lost annually in work-related diminished productivity and medical bills.

4. Leads to increased usage of alcohol and drugs.

Sleep-deprived workers may resort to alcohol and drugs as a way to compensate for fatigue. But the solution only compounds the distress. Many people wind up on a hurtling roller coaster, popping stimulants to keep awake, tossing down alcohol or sleeping pills to put themselves out, then swallowing more pills to get themselves up again. And stopping at a bar with colleagues for a postwork drink can make the situation worse: studies show that it takes less alcohol to make people drunk when they are tired.

Doctors warn that in most cases, sleeping pills should not be taken for longer than two or three weeks. Such drugs can lose their effectiveness with time, and it takes higher and higher dosages to achieve a result. People run the risk of becoming dependent on the pills.

5. Affects mental concentration, flexibility, and creativity.

Even one night of shortened sleep can produce adverse effects. People will briefly rise to an occasion, such as playing tennis or giving a speech, but mental concentration, flexibility, and creativity suffer. Two nights of skimpy sleep, and rote functioning is affected. In laboratory tests, sleep-deprived subjects have trouble adding columns of figures or doing simple repetitive tasks like hitting buttons in a prescribed pattern. Stanford researcher William Dement's studies show that if you miss sleep one night, your body keeps a record of the "sleep debt." If the debt isn't paid back soon, you'll start nodding off during the day. "We don't tend to have a good handle on our amount of sleep debt. So when we finally go bankrupt it happens fast," Dement says. "People can go from feeling wide awake to falling asleep in five seconds. If you are behind the wheel of a car, you're dead." (ibid.)

As in every aspect of our lives, there are Bible principles that apply to sleep. But if you are looking for a text saying, "Be sure to get enough rest," you may be disappointed. It seems Bible writers were more concerned with people getting too much rest! Which leads us to:

WHAT YOU CAN DO

1. Start with this "whiz quiz" to see if you are getting enough sleep:
   - Are you chronically drowsy?
   - Do you lack energy?
   - Do you need an alarm to wake up in the morning?
   - Do you fall asleep within five minutes?
   - Do you nap at will?
   If the answer to any of these questions is Yes, then you are probably short on sleep.
2. Recognize that when you overwork or play, you are living on borrowed capital—you are expending the vital force that you will need at a later time.
3. Go to bed and get up at the same time each day. Try for seven to eight hours of sleep.
4. Exercise! Steady, daily exercise deepens sleep—but only if done early. Evening exercise may disrupt sleep. So try to exercise no later

than three hours before bedtime.

5. Try reading some of the psalms from the Bible before going to bed.

6. Don't use alcohol as a sedative. It leaves the brain restless later in the night.

7. Don't do anything too stimulating just before you hope to go to sleep.

8. Avoid caffeine.

9. Set limits on your working hours.

10. Take naps.

11. Adjust your work schedule to accommodate your natural asleep/awake rhythms.

12. Consider the costs—the pay can be great for overtime or unpopular shifts, and some people prefer working miserable hours because they can get a longer stretch of time off. But is the stress to your body and mind really worth it?

FINAL THOUGHT

When there are times that for whatever reason you are unable to sleep, remember the words of Jesus in Matthew 11:28: "Come unto me, all you who labor and are heavy laden, and I will give you rest."

1. Ellen Hale, *USA Today,* 1 October 1993.

2. *Time*, 17 December 1990.

Chapter 6

THE PICK-ME-UP THAT ALWAYS LETS YOU DOWN

It seems to Joan that her husband, Jeff, is always on a deadline. Mornings are the same scenario five days a week. Jeff has trouble getting out of bed. Then by the time he finally does drag himself into the bathroom for a quick shower and shave, he's gotten himself into a rather grumpy mood.

Occasionally, Jeff gulps down a bagel, Danish, or, on rare occasions, a piece of toast. But he never misses his relished two cups of coffee, which contain the worlds most popular pick-me-up, caffeine. Jeff says the coffee really clears away the cobwebs. By the time he reaches the office, he's alert, excited, and ready to begin work.

Jeff doesn't usually eat lunch. His inner drive keeps him pushing, pushing, all day long to meet those sales quotas. He fights off hunger pangs until noon, when he unwinds over his desk with a few more cups of coffee. By midafternoon, he is feeling low on energy again. This time, he turns to a Diet Coke. Working late is normal for Jeff, and when he finally comes home—usually between 7:00 p.m. and 8:00 p.m.—he often isn't hungry because he has eaten a candy bar, has drunk a Coke, or munched on snacks from the office candy machine. But then around nine, Jeff is ravenously hungry and begins rummaging around in the refrigerator and cupboards for leftovers.

Jeff sees no connection between his coffee intake and weekend headaches. He's a busy guy—too busy to worry about how what he puts into his body may be affecting his life. In fact, Jeff is not even sure that it matters. Unwittingly, Jeff has fallen into:

DELUSION 6: WHAT I DRINK IS REALLY NO BIG DEAL!

Here is some "fascinating fiction," or excuses coffee drinkers frequently give for the habit:

- There are a lot of other things you can die from. Coffee is just one of them, and not so important.
- I'm very health conscious, but one bad thing isn't really going to hurt me.
- The benefits I derive from coffee easily outweigh any risks.
- It's a habit I don't want to break . . . it picks me up, even though I must admit it lets me down.

Any controversy that exists over coffee is certainly nothing new. Composer Johann Sebastian Bach raised a firestorm in the 1700s with his *Cof-*

fee Cantata. The heroine of the opera bravely resists her father, who tries both psychology and threats to make her quit drinking coffee. Unless she has her three cups a day, the young woman sings, "misery will reduce me to a dried-up lump of mutton." Throughout the cantata, she insists that "to put me in a good frame of mind," nothing is needed but to "just pour me out some coffee!"

Two-and-a-half centuries after Bach, those who crave coffee still mostly ignore those who urge them to eschew the brew. Coffee lovers can be found everywhere in the world, but Americans are the most passionate and loyal of all. More Americans drink coffee than don't, according to generally accepted statistics, and the nation's average aficionado enjoys about three-and-a-third cups each day. The U.S. is the world's largest importer of coffee beans. Caffeine, the powerful stimulant that gives coffee drinkers their lift, is the world's most popular drug. A number of foods and drugs (including soft drinks, chocolate, teas, weight-reduction aids, cold remedies, and pain relievers) contain caffeine, an organic compound found in the seeds or leaves of certain plants. But most caffeine is consumed in coffee.

There are a number of reasons for the popularity of coffee. Within thirty to sixty minutes of drinking a cup, caffeine levels peak in the bloodstream to produce the alertness and heightened concentration so cherished by the heroine of Bach's cantata and coffee drinkers everywhere. Caffeine augments the muscles' capacity for work, postpones exhaustion, and provides a rapid boost, both mentally and physically. Even the U.S. Olympic Committee considers caffeine a "performance enhancer," and so routinely screens athletes for the drug, lest excessive amounts confer an unfair edge. Caffeine can also squelch headaches by constricting blood vessels in the head, which is why it's added to some pain relievers.

Many Christians relish that first cup of coffee in the morning, but it's not the taste they crave—it's the jolt coffee gives. Caffeine makes them feel fresh and alert, masks fatigue, brightens the mind, and increases endurance. Some claim it gives them a more rapid flow of thought, putting a razor-keen edge on their senses and cutting reaction time. With all these positives, you may be wondering (with much of the rest of the American population):

So what's wrong with a little coffee?

Coffee contains lots of caffeine, relatively speaking, and that does have its drawbacks. The mild lift provided by a cup or two of coffee can turn to anxious overstimulation after the day's fourth or fifth cup—sooner in those who are particularly sensitive to caffeine. And caffeine creates dependence; coffee drinkers who are deprived of their daily dose may suffer headaches, tiredness, anxiety, and an impaired ability to perform physical tasks. Because caffeine stimulates the brain and spinal cord, habitual overindulgence can lead to restlessness, depression, tremors, hallucinations, and insomnia.

Caffeine can also disrupt the body's normal anxiety-relieving mechanisms, and it interferes with the function of endorphins, the naturally occurring opiates that enable us to tolerate pain and stress. It can also block the effect of prescription antidepressants and tranquilizers. Then there are some more dangerous possibilities: caffeine is suspected of causing cancer, birth defects, miscarriages, heart disease, and high blood pressure.

While not all of the studies have been totally conclusive, enough evidence has emerged on these matters to warrant further study—and to serve as a warning of the possible long-term, negative effects caffeine can have on health.

Possibly one of the most damaging arguments against coffee drinking is its addictive nature. In a recent study reported by *The Journal of the American Medical Association* (*JAMA*), 82 percent of coffee drinking adults in a study had withdrawal symptoms when they gave it up cold turkey. After going a few hours without caffeine, they became lethargic, irritable, depressed, and anxious, and they complained of headaches. Some said their symptoms were "worse than the flu." These symptoms usually take place within twelve to twenty-four hours after the last cup of coffee, then peak about twenty to forty-eight hours after the last caffeine hit.

Most often, people who drink a cup or two of coffee in the morning suffer their nastiest symptoms when they are unable to get their brew. Virtually all caffeine is eliminated from the body twelve to twenty-four hours after it was last consumed.

If you drink coffee at work during the week and have headaches on the weekends, you may be suffering from caffeine withdrawal. For years, doctors thought the nagging weekend headaches experienced by many patients signaled problems at home. But as it turned out, the headaches were actually due to caffeine withdrawal, because people weren't drinking as much coffee away from work.

In a recent study sponsored by the National Institute on Drug Abuse, researchers looked at a group of subjects who use caffeine regularly and had tried to kick the habit but couldn't. When they were deprived of their "fix," most had trouble performing their daily tasks: Two women made an unusual number of mistakes on the job; one woman called off her child's birthday party; several subjects went to bed early; and most participants said they had experienced headaches, depression or lethargy.

So what does the Bible say about caffeine?

Good question. Nothing specifically—at least in the King James Version. But there are plenty of texts that can apply. For starters, how about 2 Peter 2:19: "Of whom a man is overcome, of the same is he brought in bondage"?

Any addiction that has the power to make us depressed, jittery, lethargic, and irritable could easily fit under the description of some sort of bondage. It stands to reason that if we are to be free in Christ, that includes freedom from addiction to various stimulants—including caffeine.

If we would have clear minds, centered on Christ, we must not be buffeted by addictions and accidental withdrawals. "Whether therefore ye eat, or drink, or whatsoever ye do, do all to the glory of God" (1 Corinthians 10:31).

WHAT YOU CAN DO

If you find yourself with a caffeine addiction and are wondering what steps can help you break it, here are some ideas for places to start:

- Be sure to eat a balanced diet. What you eat in the morning can have a big effect on your performance in the afternoon. A breakfast of complex carbohydrates and protein can help fill the gap formerly filled by caffeine in the afternoon.

- Listen to the rhythms of the body. If you are a night person and recognize that you have a difficult time coming alive in the early hours of the day, do less demanding work during your down time. But seek to make a reasonable schedule for yourself, and stick to it. Go to bed at regular hours, and eat at predetermined times every day. Regularity works with the rhythmic processes of life. Nature's many voices proclaim it each day with the dawning of a new day and the setting of the sun.

- Make exercise a regular part of your day and routine. Exercise will help you relax and keep your nerves free from stress, which contributes to caffeine addiction. Relaxation exercises are excellent ways to relieve stress and avoid the use of artificial stimulants. Short naps during the day also have a restorative effect.

· Cut back gradually—perhaps by half a cup a day—or substitute a weaker beverage, such as tea or cocoa, to help reduce or prevent with drawal symptoms. If you really like the taste of coffee, switch to instant coffee or drink a half-decaffeinated blend. If tea is your source of caffeine, substitute brewed green or instant tea for brewed black.

· Check over-the-counter and prescription medications for their caffeine content. Diet preparations and many analgesics contain caffeine. Limit your intake of chocolate, cocoa, and soft drinks containing caffeine.

· Be aware of the factors that can affect your sensitivity to caffeine: age, tolerance, and personal factors. Older people are more sensitive to caffeine.

· Remember the words of Confucius: "The longest journey begins with a single step."

1. "Caffeine Dependence Syndrome," *The Journal of the American Medical Association* (*JAMA*), 5 October 1994.

Chapter 7

THE POWER TO CHANGE

Remember my story of Julie at the beginning of this book? She's the soap-opera heroine who deceptively captivated my mind. I said goodbye to her, but not without a struggle. I'd grown fond of Julie, and yet I recognized that her sterile friendship was contributing to a downward trend in my spiritual life. And for several months, the Holy Spirit convicted me that my visits with this worldly woman must end. But yet I didn't want to give up the excitement, the glamour, this character portrayed.

In my case, I'm positive the Holy Spirit gave me the desire to change. Because I don't ever remember praying about my television watching. I just recall running across an editorial in *These Times* magazine suggesting that families consider a TV blackout if they had an addiction to the "tube."

As a church leader at the time, I challenged our

entire congregation to try breaking themselves of the TV habit. As a result of those efforts, several families did make commitments to try a one-month TV blackout.

As I look back now, I am amazed at how diplomatically the Holy Spirit works. I thought at the time it was my idea. But looking back and thinking through the change in my lifestyle, I realize that the Holy Spirit is very gentle. No force. No arm twisting. Just a gentle, persistent wooing of the heart.

At the beginning of my experiment to end unholy practices in my life, I was unsure how to go about breaking a bad habit. In my case, I had to employ a step-by-step strategy, then deliberately, with determination, carry out my resolve. Perhaps as you have read this book you've begun thinking there are areas in your life that could be considered "danger zones." If that is the case, and you find there are some difficult changes you would like to make, don't be discouraged. After all, recognizing danger is the first step toward avoiding it.

We can all sympathize with Paul in the book of Romans, where he wrote, "I do not understand my own actions. For I do not do what I want, but I do the very thing I hate" (Romans 7:15, RSV). Changing the way we act has been one of the biggest challenges faced by humans in this earth's history. Too often, people have been told by others that they must change. At the same time, they have not been given any tools with which to make a turnaround. The end result is frustration. In fact, asking someone to change without telling them how (or empowering them to do it) is one of the cruelest things we can do. Fortunately, we know from the Bible that God would never expect a "redirection" in our lives without His supernatural help.

"No temptation has overtaken you except such as is common to man; but God is faithful, who will not allow you to be tempted beyond what you are able, but with the temptation will also make the way of escape, that you may be able to bear it" (1 Corinthians. 10:13, NKJV). So if we recognize that we need to make some changes in our lives, how do we change? There are several key steps to any lasting change:

Step 1: We must develop a desire for change.

As already mentioned, getting rid of my TV habit was not originally my idea. The Holy Spirit convicted me. However, I do believe that within my heart was a definite response to God. I truly wanted to please Him. I prayed to Him and read His Word.

Now, for any lasting change to take place, from the "inside out," we must have the desire to be different. As we spend time with God and obey His voice, He will send the Holy Spirit to tell us what we need to do. It is true that we sometimes do the "right thing for the wrong reasons." However, the very best scenario is to be doing the right things for the right reasons because that's what we want to do anyway. Listening to the Holy Spirit, then acting on an impression, is the first step toward that goal.

Two of the best ways to receive inspiration to make lasting lifestyle changes are Bible study and prayer. Inspiration for change may also arrive in other, less expected ways, such as in the shining example of someone you admire or books and magazines that trigger a response in your heart.

Just remember that people can't always be trusted as "shining examples." The Bible is the true guide of life. If you realize a need to change but have no desire to do it, commit yourself fully to God. Spend time with Him in Bible study and prayer, and ask Him to guide you into a deeper understanding of any changes you should make.

Step 2: We must be aware of the attitudes behind the lifestyle habits we choose to change.

Many of us have "habit groups" that just seem to go together. Like munching junk food, avoiding exercise, and excessively watching TV. Or procrastination coupled with late nights on the job and a cup of coffee to keep us awake at night and jolt us out of bed in the morning. For this reason, getting rid of one habit frequently requires that we tackle supportive habits as well.

The American Heritage Dictionary defines habit as a "constant, often unconscious inclination to perform some act, acquired through its frequent repetition. Habit applies to any activity so well established that it occurs without thought on the part of an individual."

Psychology has loosely divided our minds into two sections—conscious and subconscious. These might appear to be separate, but they make up the whole of the mind. We have control over our conscious minds but no control over our subconscious. Our conscious mind's strongest characteristic is its ability to form habits. These habits are not formed overnight, nor are they broken easily. The more frequently you do something, the more likely that it is a habit or soon will be. Everything we have ever heard, seen, thought, or acted upon filters through our subconscious mind.

Trying to understand where the attitudes behind our habits come from can be extremely helpful. Sometimes less-than-desirable habits are a reaction to people or life experiences.

For example, a friend of mine recently told me that a number of her relatives were raised in some degree of poverty during the Great Depression. At least three of them had personality traits that she felt might be attributed to their experiences during such tight times. For instance, one had a tendency to ration food, while another loved to dish out more as fast as her guests could eat. One saw great value in scraps of wood and metal; another frugally saved the same piece of aluminum foil for twenty years (or so it seemed).

Each of these people responded to their childhood hardships in a personal way—but there was a response. Our lifestyle choices are also frequently influenced by people we knew or experiences we had. And although understanding "where we are coming from" won't cure any bad choices we make, it may help us to sort things out.

Step 3: Weaken unhealthy support systems.

When I decided to replace my bad habit and attitudes with new ones, I removed the support system for my habit by finding other things to do, removing the TV from the living room, and asking God for strength and guidance. Over time, I found that the memories, activities, and relationships I had cherished for so long were fading.

If you have a lifestyle habit you would like to change, try replacing it with a good habit. You might play the piano instead of eating. Or take a walk. Call a friend. Read your Bible or another good book. Take your family for a picnic. The possibilities are really endless here, although coming up with good ideas may require some time and thought on your part.

Whatever the lifestyle change(s) that you feel

impressed to make, rest assured that God will bless your efforts. When our minds become tuned into the "heavenly channel," God will communicate with us. And when the channel is clear, so much more can be accomplished for Him. He will send supernatural help, if we call out in our weakness. God can alter our motives and even take away the desire for behaviors that sabotage our Christian walk. And when God changes us on the inside, our behavior changes on the outside.

Jesus is coming very soon. Satan knows this is true, and he would like nothing better than to obstruct our ability to think. He is the mastermind behind the toxic trends described in this book and many more that are sweeping around the world with a deadly flourish.

But the good news is that God is bigger than our enemy. Having died for us, He also loves us with an everlasting love and wants nothing more than to see us live forever in a perfect paradise.

Won't you make a commitment to be ready when our Lord appears in the heavens? One way to prepare for His soon appearing is to keep your mind as clear as possible. Every step in life—including any steps you take toward having a clearer mind—can be a step closer to Jesus, made in the firm assurance that "hitherto hath the Lord helped us" (1 Samuel 7:12), and He will help us to the end.